AROUND
CALNE
IN OLD PHOTOGRAPHS

CALNE'S CENTRAL GARDEN in about 1910. This was the site of the old Town Hall until it was demolished in 1883, after which the gardens were laid out. Edward Maundrell (see page 148) cast the ornamental iron railings which surrounded the garden, a task of some technical difficulty because the slope had to be accommodated and they were made to measure. They, like much other fine ironwork, were unnecessary victims of the salvage drive in the Second World War. High Street is in the foreground, Market Hill on the left and West Hill on the right. The name West Hill was transferred to the new stretch of the A4 which was bulldozed through the central gardens and the building on the right in 1968. The other buildings in the picture remain largely unchanged.

AROUND CALNE

IN OLD PHOTOGRAPHS

COLLECTED BY

PETER Q. TRELOAR

ALAN SUTTON

Alan Sutton Publishing Limited
Phoenix Mill · Far Thrupp · Stroud · Gloucestershire

First published 1990

British Library Cataloguing in Publication Data

Around Calne in old photographs
1. Wiltshire. Calne, history
I. Treloar, Peter Q. *1936–*
942.312

ISBN 0-86299-622-8

Typeset in 9/10 Korinna.
Typesetting and origination by
Alan Sutton Publishing Limited.
Printed in Great Britain by
Dotesios Printers Limited.

CONTENTS

ONE OF THE MAGNIFICENT STALLIONS of Cumbers' Yatesbury Shire Stud being groomed by Charlie Burgess, left, and Fred Preston (see page 96).

INTRODUCTION

This is the fourth book of photographs of Calne with which I have been concerned, all the others having been sponsored and published by the Calne Borough or Town Council. Details of them are given in the acknowledgements at the rear of this book. The latest, *Greetings from Calne*, came out in 1988 and I have cross-referenced one or two of the pictures in this book to it.

When I was asked to compile *Around Calne in Old Photographs*, I wondered whether I would have difficulty finding enough new material on the town. I need not have worried. I had a fair amount already to hand and have come across an amazing number of new photographs. In addition I was asked for the first time to cover the villages around Calne, so a whole new field was opened up and in the end I had no difficulty in assembling three hundred or more photographs from which to choose the selection in this book. Hardly any have been published before.

There is generally speaking much less old photographic material available for the villages than for the town. No doubt that was because the early photographers lived in Calne and only went out into the villages for special assignments. The coverage of the villages is inevitably very uneven because I have had to depend on the availability of material. With Compton Bassett I was lucky, in that an excellent exhibition was arranged by the community in the village during the time I was preparing the book. The exhibition showed a great deal of interesting historic material, including many photographs which have largely provided the section on Compton Bassett in this book. Other villages have had to depend on items I happen to have in my collection, what I could find from going through the stalls of postcard dealers, and what is available in public collections. I am sorry that the treatment of the villages is patchy, but I hope that the feel of the whole of the rural area surrounding Calne is conveyed. The book takes in Calne Within and Without and the surrounding parishes, including the villages of Cherhill, Yatesbury, Heddington, Sandy Lane, Derry Hill, Bremhill, Hilmarton, Lyneham and Braden-stoke.

The history of Calne can be traced back to 955 when the first mention of it is found in the will of King Edred. The most celebrated event in Calne's history occurred during the Anglo-Saxon period when in 978 at a Council of the Kingdom, the building collapsed during a debate on clerical celibacy and many were killed or injured, Archbishop Dunstan surviving by supporting himself on a beam.

Later history was largely uneventful. Calne was in the centre of the West of England woollen trade. It was recorded as early as 1189 that Stanley Abbey had erected a fulling mill for the treatment of cloth, one of the earliest known. The industry continued to expand until the Elizabethan period, by which time it accounted for nearly eighty per cent of the country's exports. Many of the mills in the Marden Valley were used for fulling, often changing to corn grinding or other uses at a later date. The woollen industry continued to be important in Calne until the early nineteenth century and it was only after that date that the bacon industry became significant, so wool was vital to Calne's economy for perhaps 600 years, bacon for only 150 or so. The bacon factory has gone, but many fine buildings of the woollen era survive on The Green and elsewhere.

The municipal history of Calne is shrouded in obscurity. The town had no proper charter until the nineteenth century, being ruled from Tudor times by two guild stewards who were elected annually and carried out whatever administrative work had to be done. The town became a 'rotten borough', its two MPs elected by a small self-perpetuating body of Burgesses who profited greatly from their votes at election time. Both town council and parliamentary elections were reformed in the 1830s, a new properly constituted council being established and the two Members of Parliament being replaced by a single one elected on a wider franchise. Thereafter the town was governed by the Borough Council which gradually acquired increasing powers over the years until its regrettable abolition in the local government changes of 1974.

Calne is reputed to have had a castle in medieval times, but virtually nothing is known about it apart from the name of the castle perpetuated in Castle House and Castle Street. During the Civil War period, on 13 July 1643, the Battle of Roundway Down was fought on the hills just above the town, and there was skirmishing in the town two years later. In recent times, Calne was a centre of military activity during the two World Wars through the presence of the Royal Flying Corps at Yatesbury in the First World War (well illustrated in this book) and the Radio Schools at Yatesbury and Compton Bassett in the Second World War, during which the aerodrome was established at Lyneham which continues to play such an important part in the defence of the country and the economy of the area.

In this book I have started at the centre of Calne and worked outwards, then taken the villages in a clockwise sweep starting with Compton Bassett. The coverage ranges from the River Marden valley to the heights of the downs, and from the glories of Bowood to humble thatched cottages. There is a section on military activity, which covers not only the regular forces of two World Wars but the Calne Volunteers of Victoria's time and the Home Guard of our own.

Transport is always a fascinating study and all forms of transport during the photographic era are well covered, from donkey-cart to railway and charabanc. The section on commerce illustrates the vitality of the local economy in Calne in the early years of the century and between the wars, much of which seems to have been sapped away by the forces of centralization and the destruction of the town centre in more recent years. The final section on agriculture depicts the industry on which Calne was largely dependent until after the Second World War, and which it continues to serve in many ways to this day.

The most significant event in recent years has been the closure and demolition of the Harris factory in the centre of Calne, followed by long debate as to what should be done in the town centre. Plans are now well advanced for a new centre incorporating a market place and riverside walk and gardens, which it is hoped will transform the town and re-establish the heart which was knocked out of it by successive enlargements of the Harris factories, and roadworks. As this book records, much of interest in Calne and its surroundings has been lost, but a great many fine and historic buildings and a wealth of beautiful scenery remain. It is to be hoped that with its heart rebuilt Calne will once again take its place as the true centre of its area, as it was when it had its own market, its own railway, its own iron foundry and the shops, services and administrative facilities needed to serve its rural hinterland.

Central Calne

AN EARLY TWENTIETH-CENTURY VIEW ACROSS THE STRAND looking towards the High Street with the Town Hall on the left. The Strand was still used as a market place at that time so the name Market Place (at the bottom of the original card) may have been the one by which it was then generally known.

AN UNCLUTTERED POSTCARD PHOTOGRAPH OF THE TOWN HALL as it was early this century. The card was posted on 11 May 1907. The Town Hall was constructed on the site of the old Town Mill and opened on 27 July 1886. (See *Greetings from Calne* : 6)

WHAT MUST BE AN EARLY POST-WAR VIEW OF THE STRAND with the Town Hall and, on the right, the Lansdowne Arms Hotel, then owned by Trust House.

ANOTHER VIEW LOOKING WEST ACROSS THE STRAND from the Harris factory. It seems to be a 1920s view with quite a large collection of motor vehicles for the period.

THE BUS must be of 1930s vintage so this is a slightly later shot showing the Lansdowne Arms being repainted. The Lansdowne Arms is one of Calne's finest surviving buildings. In addition to its long Georgian (and earlier) frontage to The Strand, it has a good range of outbuildings at the back, which once included a brewery. The central arch, which now forms the main entrance to the hotel, was once a vehicular approach to the yard. The unusual barometer set in the front wall at first-storey level is prominent in both the above pictures.

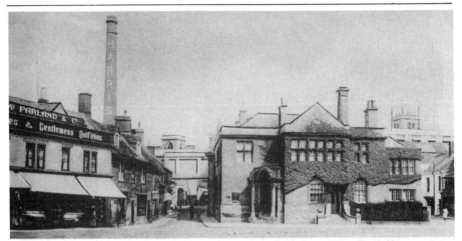

LOOKING ACROSS THE STRAND from the Lansdowne Arms with the existing Bank House, centre, but earlier Harris factory buildings than those which were recently demolished. The tower of St Mary's parish church can be seen above the factory building on the right and the tower of the Free Church just appears above the bridge over Church Street at centre.

THIS BUILDING FACING THE STRAND survived when its neighbouring buildings in Church Street (visible in the top picture) were demolished, but it remained in the ownership of Harris's and was sold with the other Harris property to the North Wiltshire District Council when the factories closed. Some thought was given to retaining it, but because of its poor condition it was demolished at the same time as the factories. The building suffered many changes of ownership and appearance over the years, as a comparison of the top and bottom pictures on this page shows. That it once comprised two separate units can be seen from the change in the size of the slates on the roof in the bottom picture.

AN EDWARDIAN PICTURE OF THE BOTTOM OF THE HIGH STREET when Buckeridge's grocery already existed on the right, where a corner of the town garden is visible (see frontispiece). This picture formed the top half of a vertical card with the Calne shield inset in the centre.

A 1950s VIEW OF THE BOTTOM END OF THE HIGH STREET with Buckeridge's shop still there, a somewhat modified town garden and the 1920 building of the Harris factory prominent in the background.

A CLOSE-UP OF THE CORNER OF BUCKERIDGE'S SHOP taken on 7 October 1921. The shop then belonged to Mr Lancelot John Buckeridge whose son, Mr John Buckeridge, comments that his mother, Louisa Jane, liked fresh air – as shown by the open windows. He identified the people in the doorway as, in the centre, Bill Corderoy (his father's cousin), with on the left Miss Brownjohn from Castle Street and on the right Miss Gladys Butler from Quemerford, with the two errand boys further right.

MOVING FURTHER UP HIGH STREET, with West Hill on the right and the town garden with Market Hill beyond in the centre. This card was posted on 12 January 1910.

A POST-SECOND WORLD WAR PICTURE of the same scene showing the town garden as it was before it was swept away by the 1968 road works.

ANOTHER POST-WAR VIEW from the top of the High Street showing a long forgotten zebra crossing outside the Kings Arms at a time when this part of High Street still formed part of the A4.

ALDRICK & NORRIS,

High St., CALNE, Wilts.

IN EDWARDIAN TIMES Aldrick and Norris occupied the shop opposite Buckeridge's towards the bottom of the High Street. It can be identified by its series of five windows in the photograph at the top of the page.

16

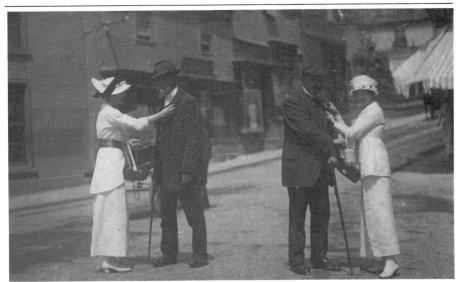

THE FIRST EARL HAIG POPPY DAY after the First World War. The picture was taken at the bottom of the High Street and the background has interesting detail of the old buildings which were subsequently taken over and altered by Midland Bank (see page 11). The ladies are, on the right, Edith Priscilla Maundrell (Mrs Johanus Sorensen) and her sister Louisa Jane Buckeridge. The gentlemen receiving poppies are, on the left, Jim Ferris and on the right, Ted Parsons.

HENLY'S GROCERY STORE at the junction of West Hill and High Street decorated for the Silver Jubilee of King George V in 1935. The building was demolished to make way for the A4 diversion in 1968.

AN EARLY PHOTOGRAPH OF CURZON STREET. The building on the right became part of the Calne Co-operative Society premises and was demolished to make way for the modern curve-fronted building which still exists, although it is no longer in the ownership of the Co-operative Society, which was constructed in the late 1930s (see p. 145). The building occupied by Webb's shop on the left was replaced by the new post office after the war. The A4 diversion runs through the site of the buildings in the centre distance.

FURTHER ALONG CURZON STREET. The cottages on the right, although much altered, still exist. Coopers' Garage is on the site of the house on the left. St Mary's Girls' Public School now occupies the land behind the cottages and trees on the right, having moved to this site from The Green in 1908. The cottage (dead centre) has disappeared.

A VIEW ACROSS THE STRAND to a military convoy driving up High Street, probably shortly before the Second World War. Taken by Miss Connie Petherick, who lived at Bank House.

ANOTHER VIEW OF THE FIRST COLLECTION for the Earl Haig Poppy Fund in 1919 or 1920. This was taken in Church Street, showing in the background the shops which then existed on the north side of the street leading into The Strand. Mr John Buckeridge records that the seller was Frances Ogg who married Dick Dew, farmer, of Scotts Farm, Stockley.

THIS CARD WAS POSTED on 25 August 1950 and shows the post-war appearance of Church Street before Wiltshire's store on the left was demolished to make way for the first supermarket on the site. Subsequently it was replaced by the much larger supermarket and shops which now exist in Mill Street, from which the elderly car is emerging in the picture.

A VIEW LOOKING NORTH-WESTWARD FROM THE CHURCH TOWER in the early years of the century. On the right is the Free Church, and behind it the older buildings of the Harris factory. Traces of the building immediately beyond the Free Church survived until the recent demolition of the factory. In the immediate foreground are the roofs of the buildings which lined Mill Street, including Wiltshire's store appearing in the picture at the top of the page. The row of shops in Church Street is complete and in the distance (top left) the Workhouse building in what is now the grounds of St Mary's School can just be made out.

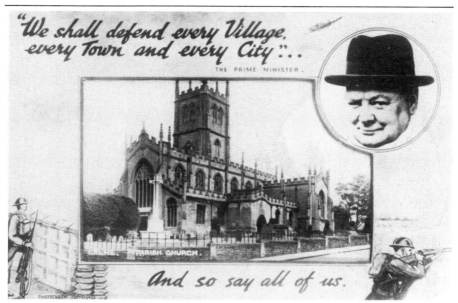

A PATRIOTIC POSTCARD, no doubt produced in the darkest days of the Second World War in 1940.

AN EXCELLENT INTERIOR PHOTOGRAPH OF ST MARY'S PARISH CHURCH taken about 1890. The nearer pillars and arches of the nave are Norman work of the twelfth century. Beyond them, the crossing had to be rebuilt when the tower fell and destroyed the centre of the church on 26 September 1638. The clerestory or upper windows of the nave and the roof are of the late fifteenth century. The decoration above the arch at the end of the nave, apparently nineteenth century, has since been painted over. After the date of the picture, the roof of the chancel was raised and a taller window inserted in the east end.

THE FREE CHURCH in Church Street. In 1866 a rift developed in the congregation of St Mary's parish church between those with what may be loosely called Low- and High-Church views. The views and actions of the Reverend John Duncan, who was inducted in 1865, upset a considerable number of his congregation, including the Harris and other influential families. In 1866 the disaffected party formed a separate congregation who worshipped at first in the Town Hall. The foundation stone of their church was laid a short distance down Church Street from the parish church on 29 October 1867 and it was completed on 28 July 1868. The architect was Mr Stent of Warminster. The church has always been controlled by its congregation and has remained entirely separate from other denominations. The postcard is undated. It may be from the period between the wars. The front wall and railings are intact and there is a heavy growth of ivy, which has since been removed.

NOTHING IS KNOWN of this delightful Victorian portrait other than what the inscription says, that it was taken by a photographer called Porter of Church Street, Calne.

Calne: Away from the Centre

THE BEST KNOWN MINISTER of the Calne Free Church was the Reverend Robert Wheeler who was minister from 1879 to 1930. He was an excellent amateur photographer and took this photograph of the River Marden showing his house at No. 1 The Green on the left and the parish church on the right, with his family and friends in the foreground and his vegetable garden beyond. (See also page 30.)

A LAST GLIMPSE OF THE PALACE CINEMA and other buildings in Mill Street before they were demolished to make way for the new supermarket and office block in the early 1970s. As this picture shows, the cinema had an impressive façade to Mill Street, which hid little more than a tin-roofed shed behind. The original appearance of the façade was considerably more attractive (see *Greetings from Calne* : 86).

LOOKING UP THE RIVER MARDEN from the northernmost of the two bridges in Mill Street. This shows the water held at full height for working the mill which stands behind the photographer. The cottage on the right was rare in Calne, being both largely timber-framed *and* thatched. The thatch had been replaced by tiles by the time it was demolished in the 1970s to make way for the house which temporarily became the new vicarage. (For a frontal view see *Greetings from Calne* : 81.)

AN EDWARDIAN SCENE IN MILL STREET with posed children. This formed the left half of a double card with shield at centre. The mill is on the right, and the cottages on the left nearest the camera were demolished to make way for improvements to the course of the river after the 1920 flood. The card was posted on 2 July 1909 and carried the message 'Here's a bit of old Calne. We have a fine old Church.'

TWO OF THE ALMSPEOPLE outside the almshouses in Kingsbury Street. Another photograph taken by the Reverend Wheeler, who lived opposite the almshouses. The almshouses were provided by Dr John Tounson, who was vicar of Bremhill at the time of the Civil War, and are said to have been given by him to commemorate the recovery of his living at the Restoration. The inscription on the building reads, in part, 'To the Glory of God and the good of the poore was this house erected by John Tounson Dr D. son of Robert late Bishop of Salisbury 1682'. There were originally eight almshouses for occupation by widows. The class of occupants has since been widened and in the 1960s the eight houses were converted into four more roomy units.

AN EDWARDIAN COUPLE who contrast starkly with the two widows of the same era pictured above. This series of these cards was no doubt considered rather saucy at the time. The figures were superimposed on the background scene, in this case The Green.

AN EDWARDIAN POSTCARD OF THE GREEN. The children would have been attending the schools which at that time were concentrated on The Green, being the Boys' and Girls' National Junior Schools, the Grammar School (just visible extreme left) and the Technical School. It is apparent that The Green comprised much more gravel than grass at that time.

THE GREEN, CALNE

K 3012

A POST-WAR VIEW looking towards the northern corner of The Green, showing pavement under construction. The buildings have remained largely unchanged, the only significant alteration being the conversion of the building at left centre to flats, which occurred in the 1970s. It was built originally as a wool factory but by the time of the photograph was being used as a sawdust store by Harris's.

BOSTOCK AND WOMBWELL'S TRAVELLING ZOO set up on The Green some time in the 1920s. A central arena was formed between two lines of trailers like the one shown, linked by the canvas roof. The trailer trains were hauled by traction engines, of which two are visible.

ANOTHER EDWARDIAN VIEW OF THE GREEN seen from the junction with London Road. The school children are again present and there is a nice period lamp post. Note, outside the Boys' School on the left, the Crimean War cannon and the drinking fountain. The cannon was presented to the town in 1858 and was removed for scrap during the Second World War (see *Greetings from Calne* : 3 and 70).

THIS ENORMOUS BONFIRE was built to celebrate
the coronation in 1937. It was almost certainly
on The Green and makes an interesting
comparison with the one built there for the
Silver Jubilee in 1935 (illustrated in *Greetings
from Calne* : 30). The 1937 builders obviou-
sly set out to make an even bigger and better
bonfire than the 1935 one. It must have made
a dramatic blaze.

A NINETEENTH-CENTURY PORTRAIT CARD of
a Salvation Army member of whom,
again, nothing is known except that he
was photographed by G. Colwell of The
Green, Calne. There is further reference
to the Salvation Army on pages 38 and
49.

ANOTHER OF THE REVEREND WHEELER'S PICTURES, taken from approximately where the children are standing in the picture on page 23. Behind his two daughters in the punt are the hatches which controlled the supply of water to the mill in Mill Street to the left. Anchor Road runs along the skyline, free of the council houses built between the wars. The Recreation Ground Lodge is the building on the left.

Q.IV.20

THE FLOOD of 9 April 1920 (helpfully written on the postcard) fills New Road. It was probably after this event that the arches were inserted in the wall on the left to allow easier escape of the water, should flooding recur. On the right the 1920 wing of the Harris factory is under construction.

THE PUBLIC LIBRARY in New Road was built in 1904 and bears the following inscriptions: 'This building is the gift of Andrew Carnegie' and 'This stone was laid July 16th 1904 by the Earl of Kerry'. There is a fine carving of the Borough coat of arms in the gable over the doorway. The site of the 1920 wing of the Harris factory is still covered in trees and bushes, with just a fragment of the older factory building visible beyond the library.

LOOKING ALONG THE RIVER MARDEN AND NEW ROAD, probably in the 1920s, soon after the construction of the Harris factory. The backs of the Great Western Railway's notice boards at the entrance to Station Road can be seen on the right. The building on the left is Marden House, currently in course of renovation as a Community and Arts Centre. Of the bridges over the river, the nearer footbridge has been removed and the two-arch bridge beyond has been replaced by a single straight span.

River Marden, Calne   I am simply "held" by the charms her

THE SAME VIEWPOINT, with the superimposed Edwardian courting couple. Note how the telegraph pole sprouted extra insulators between the Edwardian and 1920s views. The Calne branch of the Wilts. and Berks. Canal joined the river just to the left of the photographer. It opened in 1802 and was out of use by 1900. Barges making for the wharf beyond the bridge had to squeeze through the larger arch in the background.

ONLY THE ADDRESS could be written on the back of postcards until 1902, so any message had to be written on the same side as the picture. This card was posted in Calne on 30 September 1903 to Mrs Norris of Oxford Villas, Calne. The backward-written message reads: 'I wonder how you are now? Hope all the colds have taken their departure before this. Shall come and see you the first chance I have. I went home for Sunday and came back again for a few more days.' Under the note about pigs it says, 'Has Mr Norris written in my album yet??? With Love'. Seen from the station area, the top lock of the canal is visible (centre) with Marden House and the earlier Harris factory chimneys beyond.

THE HIGHLANDS, now known as Vern Leaze, is a large nineteenth-century house in Silver Street in a fine position overlooking the Marden valley. It has changed little over the years although creepers are no longer allowed to run riot over the building as they were in this Edwardian view. Since the picture was taken the veranda has been removed and a wall with parapet has been built to support the terrace.

London Road, Calne.

THE GREAT WESTERN RAILWAY introduced what it called a 'motor service' between Marlborough and Calne stations on 10 October 1904. The view above shows one of the original buses driving up London Road.

LONDON ROAD, CALNE.

LOOKING IN THE OTHER DIRECTION to the upper part of London Road, probably at about the same period.

TWO MORE VIEWS OF THE UPPER END OF LONDON ROAD which probably date from the 1920s. Features of interest include the garage on the right and the tall Georgian building beyond, both of which have since disappeared to make way for a modern filling station (*Greetings from Calne*: 63–65), the gas lamps, the tall telegraph poles set at the pavement edge and the sloping gutter. The vehicle outside the garage seems to be a three-wheeler. The road surface is smooth and well cared for but it is not clear whether it has been tarmacked. In the centre of the bottom picture is a house which disappeared to make way for the haulage contractor's yard which occupied the site until 1988. Since then it has been redeveloped as a small housing estate.

THE UPPER END OF LONDON ROAD seen from the opposite direction to the views on the previous page, probably in the 1920s. On the left is Wessington Lodge which was an outer lodge for Bowood House. Traffic from the London direction could turn in here and take the short side of the triangle instead of continuing down London Road and up Silver Street to the Pillars Lodge entrance to the estate.

WESSINGTON LODGE. CALNE.

WESSINGTON LODGE in beautifully maintained condition in Edwardian times. What is fascinating about this card is that it was posted on 7 January 1910 from 6 Curzon Street, Calne 'With best wishes from us all Alice S M Henly, May Henly, Millicent Henly' and was addressed simply to 'Dr and Mrs Wheeler, Pekin, via Siberia'. Dr Wheeler was a missionary son of the Reverend Wheeler of the Free Church. The postmarks show that having been posted in Calne on 7 January it was in Pekin (overland by rail) by 20 January. The address must have been adequate, as it was no doubt Dr Wheeler who brought the card back to Calne.

Wessington Avenue, Calne.

AN EDWARDIAN POSTCARD of the lime tree avenue at Wessington, with the usual posed children of the period.

Wessington Avenue, Calne

My time has been very pleasantly filled in here

WESSINGTON AVENUE forms the background for another of the superimposed Edwardian groups. The background scene with the lady leading a donkey was produced as an ordinary postcard as well.

A POST-WAR VIEW OF WESSINGTON AVENUE. The windows in the timber-framed building on the right are said to have come from the old Workhouse building (see page 20) when it was demolished by J.H. Blackford & Son between the wars.

THE BUILDING SHOWN ABOVE had an extremely interesting history. It is described as standing in Bollings Lane, although the lane on its right is now the innermost section of Back Road. It is reported to have been built in about 1695 as a Presbyterian chapel. It later became Unitarian and so attracted Joseph Priestley when he was librarian to the Earl of Shelburne from 1773 to 1780. Priestley was a well known Unitarian and it is recorded that he often preached in the chapel. He is believed to have isolated oxygen while living in Calne, carrying out experiments in the River Marden. The chapel closed as a Unitarian chapel in the early nineteenth century but was subsequently taken over by the Primitive Methodists who in turn gave it up when they moved to a building which had formerly been an engineering works in London Road. Early in the twentieth century the Salvation Army took the chapel over as its Citadel and it became a forces' canteen during the Second World War. After that it served as an overflow classroom for the Bentley Grammar School but was demolished when work started on the Calne Borough Council's Linden Close housing development.

AN EDWARDIAN VIEW OF THE LOWER END OF QUEMERFORD showing the state of the A4 in pre-tarmac days. The houses have remained much the same to this day.

THIS POSTCARD WAS POSTED on 31 May 1907 in Calne. It says 'This is the room', but unfortunately gives no indication as to the use to which it was put. It seems to have been a chapel and stands just on the Calne side of the Jolly Miller Inn. It was converted to a dwelling-house in the 1970s. The railings (seen at the right of the top picture) must have been taken for the scrap effort during the war.

AN UNEXPLAINED AND CURIOUSLY ASSORTED GROUP outside the New Inn (which can be read on the lamp over the door). It is now the Jolly Miller, Quemerford. The name of the licensee was F. Cox and the clothing appears to be of the 1920s. Note the chimney sweep and the postman in earlier style uniform.

A MOTHER AND SON STUDY in Quemerford, perhaps in the 1920s.

SECTION THREE

Calne: People and Happenings

A SPLENDID PHOTOGRAPH OF THE CALNE SHOPPING WEEK PROCESSION of 1925 coming down the High Street, taken from Buckeridge's shop. L. & O. Hawkins on the right continued as a butchers under that name until recent years. Next to it C. Telling was a saddler's which went out of business many years ago, although the building remained in the ownership of the family until recently.

AN EARLY SCHOOL PHOTOGRAPH. This was the British School which used the schoolroom behind the Free Church in Church Street and the photograph must date from the Victorian period. The school was built at the same time as the Free Church in 1868, the intention being that it should be used as a Sunday School on Sundays and as a British School run by an independent committee with non-denominational religious teaching during the week.

A GROUP PHOTOGRAPH of the Junior School on The Green taken for the coronation in 1953. It is probably in the former Boys' School of 1829 on the corner of The Green.

SPEECH DAY at the County Secondary School in Silver Street. This must have been very soon after the school opened in 1930. It was much enlarged in 1963 and adopted the name 'Fynamore' in 1964, becoming merged in The John Bentley Comprehensive School, of which it now forms the north wing, in 1974.

THE GUTHRIE JUNIOR SCHOOL in 1928. The school was reached by a path from Wood Street. It is currently the workshop home of Calne sculptor Richard Cowdy, who designed and cast the pig sculpture in Phelps Parade. The Guthrie School was founded in 1854 and provided with new buildings in William Street in the post-war period. R.I. Butcher, third from right in the back, has identified two sisters named Richards, and twin boys named Silk who later joined the navy.

IN CONTRAST TO THE TOP PHOTOGRAPH, a group of Guthrie School children taken at a much later date, believed to be during the Second World War, with their head teacher Miss Ivy Billett.

THE ELDERLY COUPLE in this photograph have been identified as William and Charlotte Bush who died in 1912 and 1906 respectively. They are standing outside their home, at No. 28 Shelburne Road, with May Pollock and their housekeeper Elizabeth Collier. Mr and Mrs Bush had previously run the White Horse Inn and a bakery in Compton Bassett.

HENRY SILVERTHORNE BAILEY, treasurer of the Calne Co-operative Penny Bank, which always paid eleven per cent, in his garden at the back of the last cottage in the row in Curzon Street (seen at the right of the picture at the bottom of page 18).

KING EDWARD VII AND QUEEN ALEXANDRA paid a formal visit to Calne on 22 July 1907. They had been staying at Bowood and in the course of their return to London drove through Calne and accepted a ceremonial address at the Town Hall before going on to the railway station where the royal train was waiting to return them to London. The picture above shows the moment of the presentation outside the Town Hall. There is a close-up view of the Bowood carriage on page 130.

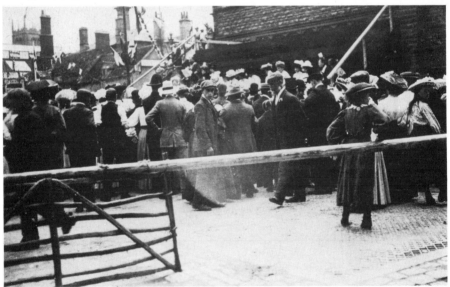

THE SCENE ON THE STRAND on the date of the royal visit, probably before it happened. Note the staging erected against the Town Hall in the background and the older Harris factory buildings with the church tower visible above them to the left. The patterned metal surface in the foreground may be a weighbridge.

ANOTHER VIEW OF THE WAITING CROWD ON THE STRAND looking up the High Street. For further pictures of the event, see the author's earlier books, in particular *Greetings from Calne* : 20, 21 and 76.

LADIES PARTICIPATING IN A DECORATED BICYCLE COMPETITION on the Recreation Ground in about 1904.

THE RECREATION GROUND LODGE again forms the background in this photograph of the post office staff, probably of the 1920s when the older style of uniform was still in use.

THE CALNE SALVATION ARMY BAND in 1908. The Bandmaster Frank Webb, centre front, lived in Alma Terrace. His father (bearded) is sitting next to him. Also in the photograph but unidentified are Frank's son Herbie, and Ernest Strange. It was an old Calne story which caused much amusement that, through a misunderstanding, on one occasion the front row of these musicians marched down New Road while the rest went down Church Street.

WHAT IS PROBABLY THE CALNE TOWN BAND playing outside the Woodlands in the inter-war period. The Woodlands was a large Italian-style house erected in the nineteenth century by one of the Harris family. It was demolished in 1983. It was used as part of the Woodlands Club, which still continues to function in older buildings on the site. The large and well-wooded grounds have been developed with housing over the last few years.

AN UNIDENTIFIED EVENT on The Strand some time in the early years of the century. Right of centre is the horse-drawn fire engine with its volunteer firemen standing on it. Marden House and old wharf buildings appear on the extreme left.

AN UNDATED PHOTOGRAPH of the crowds watching water sports on the river Marden alongside the wharf. There was such an event during the coronation celebrations in 1911 but it is not known if this is it. The people sitting across the middle of the picture are on the tin roof of one of the wharf buildings which is faced with advertisements looking out over the river. Beyond them are houses in Patford Street which have since been demolished. The spectators with their backs to the camera in the foreground are looking into the river from New Road. The trio on the centre of the roof marked with an arrow are, from left to right, Messrs Onslow Hawkins, Launcelot John Buckeridge and Levu Hawkins. Messrs Hawkins for many years ran the butchers' business in High Street (see page 41). The trio are 'the sporting fraternity' who inscribed the card at top right.

THE COMMITTEE OF THE CALNE CHAMBER OF COMMERCE in 1926. Central are Mr John and Mrs Bodinnar, behind them Bernard Dixon and on the extreme right Bertram Spackman.

THE LATE MR T.R. HOOD, who practised as a solicitor in Calne from 1932 to 1982, wrote the following note about the above picture. 'When Hitler announced his intention of incorporating the Saar in the German Reich in 1931 through the League of Nations, a referendum was announced and this was to be supervised by an unarmed body of observers. The British Legion volunteered to produce observers and the eight members of the Calne Branch shown in the photograph were selected. They embarked at Tilbury and they stood in the Thames for 24 hours during which time they were violently ill. The Saarlanders showed such unaminity for incorporation in the Reich that the plebiscite was called off and the members of the Calne British Legion returned home. They were entirely unpaid for their services.' Back row, left to right: R.A.C. Dare, J. Kelloway, J. Rutherford, M.E. Cook. Front row: R. Caswell, J.P. Shearer, R. Hill and C.E. Blackford.

AN EDWARDIAN SCENE of children dancing around a maypole on the Recreation Ground. The massed ladies on the pavilion steps in the background are wearing a superb collection of hats.

A LATER PICTURE of a maypole being carried in procession down New Road, probably in the 1920s. The curved bow window of South Place can be seen projecting into the road in the background (right). It was demolished in 1962 to make way for the improved junction with Silver Street (see *Greetings from Calne* : 85).

ALL THAT IS RECORDED OF THIS PHOTOGRAPH is that it is of the Quemerford Boys' Club. It must date from the inter-war years, and flat caps were clearly in fashion.

A GROUP OF CALNE GUIDE LEADERS photographed in the 1920s.

THE FIRST CALNE GUIDE COMPANY photographed outside the Orangery at Bowood House on 22 April 1922.

CALNE SECONDARY SCHOOL GIRLS' HOCKEY TEAM about 1904. Back row, left to right: Mabel Cleverly, Dorothy Fell, Edith Priscilla Maundrell (daughter of E.W. Maundrell of The Foundry), Dorothy Gough (sister to Mr C.O. Gough, Town Clerk), a teacher, Louisa Jane Maundrell (sister of Edith, became Mrs L.J. Buckeridge), -?-, -?-. Front row: Dorothy Keevil, Grace Rumming, Hilda Hillier, Hilda Wood, Madge Gough (sister of Dorothy), Joan Pocock, Edith Smart, Ella Mary Maundrell (sister of Edith).

THE REVD A. GRIFFITHS was minister of the London Road Primitive Methodist church from 1924 to 1932 and he is in the centre of this group of young people who took part in a tennis match between the Baptist and Methodist Church Youth on Wiltshire's Court on part of what is now the supermarket site in Mill Street. The following have been identified as being in the picture: Leslie Smith, Christine Miles, Betty Exton, Mildred Chivers, Dorothy Gail, Minnie Hitchens, Violet Shobbrook (Mrs Will Parry), Nora Chivers, Fred Burchell, Maurice Morement, Reg Gale, Roger Wiltshire and Nellie Hitchens. Of these the author can identify only Roger Wiltshire (later one of the proprietors of Wiltshire's Store in Church Street), third from the right, and Violet Shobbrook in front of him.

A BOWLING MATCH in the forecourt of the Harris factory off The Strand. The photograph is dated 1921, which was just after completion of the building on the right, the 1920 wing of the Harris factory adjoining New Road, the canopy of which is shading the bowling alley. It was not until 1930 that the remainder of the modern brick factory replaced the older buildings in the background. There is a coconut-shy behind the crowd with a sign, 'You can't miss 'em!'

ANKLE COMPETITION, Harris Carnival 1926. A nice study of footwear as well as ankles.

MR AND MRS AARON PONTING photographed at their home at Ratford Hill just outside Calne. Mr Ponting was born in 1840 and died in 1931. His wife Mary Ann (née Richens) was born in the same year and died in 1922. She came from East Tytherton and they were married in 1866.

MR ALBERT GALE digs the back garden of his home in The Pippin while his cat keeps an eye on the photographer. He built the house for his son Fred (Mayor of Calne, 1931) and daughter-in-law as a wedding present and named it Minfred House after them.

AN EDWARDIAN FAMILY GROUP, of which nothing is known except that it was taken by yet another Calne photographic studio, that of G. & E. Wiltshire.

THE WEDDING GROUP of Albert Weston and Ada Whale at 185 Quemerford on 11 June 1932. Frank Weston was best man. Others in the picture are Ernest Whale, Catherine Reeves (on lap), Mrs Maud Angell (on the left with a child) and next to her Mrs Reeves. The card is inscribed to 'Aunt Lizza from Ada and Albert'.

ONE OF THE REVD WHEELER'S PICTURES, this one showing circus elephants in New Road in the early years of the century.

AN INTERESTED CROWD examine a new ambulance delivered to Calne in 1927. The curved sign on the side says 'Borough of Calne' with the word 'Goodwill' above the cross. The mayor John Bodinnar is standing in the doorway of the Town Hall and seems to be taking formal delivery of the vehicle. The Borough Council did not run an ambulance in its later years as the responsibility passed to the National Health Service when it was formed.

THERE IS NO INFORMATION recorded about this group of Calne children but they are probably the Baptist Church Sunday School (about 1930).

A BRITISH LEGION TEA PARTY in Calne about forty years ago. Mrs K. Warner who lent the photograph explained that it included her grandchildren Carol and Clive Warner.

THE 'CALNE MODERATES' about 1912. They were an 'informal group who got around together and had a lot of fun'. Back row, from the left: Bert Granger, Bob Taylor (barber of Church Street), Frank Williams, 'Waxy' Beasley, Weston, L.J. Buckeridge. Centre row: Teddy Smith (tailor of High Street, the best breeches maker for miles around), Tickner, Faircloth, Dick Couman. Front row: Bill Corderoy, Carter.

A CALNE GROUP celebrating their man's election victory. The sign says 'N. Wilts Con Gain M. [for majority] 288'. The sign on the hat in the centre says 'Terrell, local man'. George Terrell was Unionist MP for North Wiltshire from 1910 to 1922.

A CHARMING SHOT OF THE CARNIVAL QUEEN and her attendants on their float outside the White Hart Hotel, probably in the 1930s.

THIS IS BELIEVED TO BE the opening of the new playground at the Recreation Ground c. 1931–2. Left to right: Phyllis Partridge (Whiles), who provided the names, Agneta Rutty (Puffett), Joan Thomas, Kathleen Webb, Sylvia Hewlance, Roma Barry (Lewis), Peggy Brittain, Iris Culley and Kathleen Slade (Dixon).

THE LONDON ROAD BOYS' FOOTBALL TEAM some time before 1914. The picture was provided by Mr John Lambourne whose brother George, born in 1900, played with them. George Hitchens is second from the right at the rear, and the three Lugg brothers present are Frederick (top left), Bill (top right) and Thomas (probably second left, front).

NOTHING IS KNOWN about this splendid study of Edwardian ladies except that it came from a house in Bromham and was taken by the Calne photographer J.J. Hunt.

BY WAY OF CONTRAST, a relaxed group during the coronation celebrations in 1953 in Penn Hill Road, Calne. Names recorded are: front left, Mrs J. Crocker, Mr Saye, Mr Webb; middle row, second right, Mrs V. Parry; third row, right, Mr W. Parry; rear row, Mr G. Hazel and Mr and Mrs Reeves.

A PROCESSION IN THE HIGH STREET about 1930.

THE CARNIVAL PROCESSION drives up Church Street on Coronation Day, 1937. St Mary's churchyard is at the extreme right, the low railings still in place.

ARCHDEACON BODINGTON ADDRESSING THE CROWD on The Green on Empire Day, about 1910. Canon Bodington was vicar of Calne from 1907 to 1927.

A PROCESSION ON THE GREEN about 1930. Note, as well as the children in the front of the picture, a horse-drawn cart carrying a group of children in white behind them and the town band to the right.

A CONCERT GROUP REHEARSING. Believed to have been in Quemerford, and the clothing indicates that it was taken in the inter-war years, but nothing more is known.

ELMFIELD, LICKHILL ROAD in the early years of the century with the family posed for the photographer. The house remains largely unchanged but bay windows have been added to the ground floor.

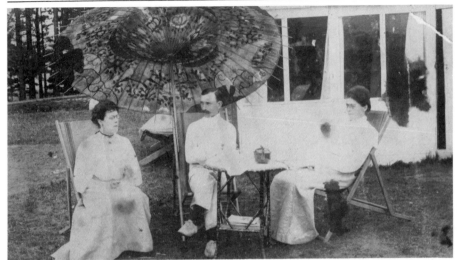

'WE THINK THIS IS A CALNE FAMILY in the town's summer "Camp" on Blacklands Downs about 1910. A "shanty" town grew up, some people having a smart hut like this one, others not so smart and some people in tents. They went here after work and at weekends. Cricket matches and other activities took place. The main encampment was in the vicinity of the present golf club house. In the end it was closed down by order of the local authority who were afraid that the primitive sanitary arrangements would cause "disease".' (John and Paul Buckeridge.)

A TABLEAU from the Coronation Day carnival procession of 1937, the three groups from the left representing 'Justice and Mercy', 'The Muse of History' and 'Jehoiada crowning Joash'. The story of the crowning of Joash can be found in II Kings, chapter 11. Joash's brothers were killed by his grandmother Athaliah who seized the throne. Joash was hidden in the temple but when he was aged seven the High Priest Jehoiada had him proclaimed King and the Queen was killed. Why was this scene chosen for the 1937 Coronation Procession? Was there an implied comment on the abdication of Edward VIII and his replacement by George VI, whose coronation was being celebrated?

Compton Bassett

Compton House, near Calne

COMPTON HOUSE WAS BUILT about 1670 by Sir John Weld. It was in the ownership of the Heneage family from 1761 until 1918. They ceased to occupy it themselves in 1902 and in 1918 the whole of the Compton Bassett and Cherhill estates was sold by the Heneage family to the Co-operative Wholesale Society. The Society in its turn sold the estates in 1929–30 and the house was demolished in 1931–33.

HOME FARM HOUSE, Compton Bassett in 1890. The house is at right angles to the road. It has since had an extension built parallel with the road, so this view is unfamiliar. The farmer Mr Hewlett and his wife pose before their house with a fine carthorse.

COMPTON BASSETT CHURCH in 1925. The gates were taken for the scrap drive during the war. Compton House still stands in the right background. The burial ground has since been extended in the foreground.

RE-ROOFING THE CHURCH, about 1950. The church has a Norman nave with additions of the Perpendicular and Victorian periods, as evidenced by the Perpendicular clerestory windows below the roof of the nave and the Victorian north porch.

COMPTON HOUSE AND GARDEN in its Edwardian glory. The group are probably members of the Heneage family.

IN CONTRAST, the other, or front, side of the house when demolition was just beginning in 1931. The house had been bought from the Co-operative Society by Captain Guy Benson in 1930. He found it uneconomic to keep up and converted the stables for use as a house in its place.

THE SCHOOL AND ADJOINING HOUSES about 1920. The distinctive and homogenous style of the houses in Compton Bassett was achieved while it was in the ownership of the Heneage family during the nineteenth century.

SCHOOL GROUP, 1928. The headmistress, Mrs Bulley, on the left and her assistant, Miss Billett, on the right. Front row, left to right: Jim Carter, Albert Goodenough, Peter Rumming, Irene Salter, Sam Rumming, Tom Smith, Betty Smith, Charlie Fell, Irene Hooper, Mildred Summers, Florence Fisher. Middle row: Margaret Smith, Doreen Goodenough, Eileen Summers, John Goodenough, Ella Mills. Back row: Kathleen Salter, Reginald Rumming (provider of much of the material about Compton Bassett in this book), Fred Evans and Charlie Summers.

THIS SPLENDID PHOTOGRAPH of the Duke of Beaufort's hounds moving off after meeting at Compton Bassett was used in the 1930 auction particulars for the Compton Bassett and Cherhill estates.

A WINTER VIEW OF THE UPPER END OF THE VILLAGE about 1930 with the White Horse Inn on the right.

A TUG OF WAR being held outside the White Horse in 1919.

A GROUP OF SCHOOLCHILDREN pose in the road at the top end of the village, with Nos 49 and 50 Compton Bassett behind them, in 1922.

LOOKING IN THE OPPOSITE DIRECTION with a donkey cart approaching and the Manor House in the distance on the left.

THE MANOR HOUSE is dated 1699 and this is the earliest known photograph of it.

MANOR COTTAGE in 1903. The Rumming family pose for their photographs. Left to right: Alice, Alma (Reg's grandmother), Mr Parker, Patricia, Jack, Bill (Reg's father) and George (Reg's grandfather). Jim is at the window.

NO. 57 COMPTON BASSETT about 1924, with Mrs Alma Rumming sitting outside. The beautifully fan-trained fruit trees are a striking feature in many old views of the village and some still survive.

A WEDDING AT NO. 57 in 1919. The bride and groom are Jack Taylor and Florence Rumming. Almost everyone else in the photograph was a member of the Rumming family. Note the footpath of Calne cobbles, hard limestone cobbles of a distinctive type which seem to be found only in Calne and a few of the surrounding villages.

GAMEKEEPER BILL RUMMING, who was keeper of the Compton Estate in CWS days when the shooting was let to a Colonel Pope. His son Reg is with him.

THE VILLAGE POND in 1924.

THE OLDEST PHOTOGRAPH in the book. Recorded on the original as having been taken in 1859, it shows the girl who became Mrs Alma Rumming (1854–1938).

AN EARLY TWENTIETH-CENTURY STUDY of four of the Rumming children at No. 60 Compton Bassett. The girl on the left is now Mrs Min Godwin, aged eighty-five, behind her is Alice and the others are Bill and Hilda. There were nine children altogether in the family.

Evening Advertiser   **Swindon Advertiser**

DR TO **A. GOODENOUGH**

WHEELWRIGHT, UNDERTAKER AND GENERAL SMITH

COMPTON BASSETT

M .... 19......

Funeral expenses of the late HANNAH RUMMING
who died 8th November 1938 aged 71 Years
Buried at Highway Churchyard November 12th 1938

Pannelled Polished Elm Coffin with Brass
Fittings Swanette linings and Silk Lace
with Shroud to match 6 Brass Wreath
Holders also Double Capped   £8 0 0

4 Bearers at 3/- each   12 0
Church Bells and Grave expenses   12 6

£9 4 6

A. J. GOODENOUGH

BEARERS.
L. WALT LEWIS   R. BILL FELL
JACK RUMMING   CHARLIE LEWIS.

GOODENOUGH'S BILL FOR THE FUNERAL OF HANNAH RUMMING on 12 November 1938. She was one of the last people to be buried in Highway churchyard before it was closed. This is a fascinating piece of social history, starting with the detail of the activities of a general smith in a country village in the 1930s (it must even then have been unusual to have newspapers advertised on funeral accounts), showing the low cost of a funeral in those days and even containing pictures of the undertaker, the manually propelled hearse and the bearers.

SECTION FIVE

South-east of Calne: Cherhill to Yatesbury

THE INTERIOR OF THE GREAT TITHE BARN at Cherhill. This view shows the upright timbers which were probably inserted at some stage in the barn's history to support the great curved cruck timbers which originally provided the sole support for the massive stone-tiled roof.

Old Tithe Barn Cherhill. Near Calne.

THE TITHE BARN seen from the church (above) and road sides. The barn was 110 ft long and the pictures show the two porches on each side and the rather unusual hipped roof design with its covering of stone tiles. Another unusual feature was the upright oak studding which formed the greater part of the walls above the stone plinth. It is visible on the right in the interior picture overleaf and in the top picture. It is believed that the barn was constructed in the fifteenth century. A date of 1425 is said to have been discovered on a timber during repairs in 1868. Constructed originally to house the one-tenth of farm produce payable to the Church, it eventually became the barn of The Manor and served that purpose until The Manor and the farm were split on the Co-operative Wholesale Society sale in 1929. Thereafter it never found another use and because of its deterioration and the expense of restoring it, was demolished in 1956. A great loss, as had it survived a few more years, means would surely have been found to preserve it.

CHERHILL MANOR AND CHURCH c. 1929. The church is largely in the Perpendicular style. The Manor House was greatly altered to its disadvantage in the nineteenth century when it lost much of its character as a typical stone-built large house of about the Elizabethan period.

A MEET OF THE HUNT outside the Black Horse Inn at Cherhill. The Inn has since been extended to the right and the thatched barn has disappeared. The quiet country road in the foreground is hardly recognizable as the wide and busy tarmacked A4 of today. The manorial records show that the original part of the inn was built between 1765 and 1768. Taken from a card posted on 25 November 1907.

THIS EARLY TWENTIETH-CENTURY VIEW shows the Post Office Stores in Cherhill, identifiable by the post box at the extreme left end of the building. The post box, bearing the insignia 'V.R.', is still there, but the building has been greatly changed. The stone tiles on the roof have been replaced by modern manufactured tiles and the windows by metal-framed ones. However, it is still the post office.

A VIEW IN THE STREET AT CHERHILL with the school, Manor House and church. The school building shown was built during the second quarter of the nineteenth century. It has since been refaced, with the insertion of a dormer. The card was posted in Cherhill, some time before the First World War, to Bath, with the usual confident expectation that the news of the sender's plans for the next day would reach the receiver in time.

AN EARLY TWENTIETH-CENTURY VIEW OF CHERHILL looking south over The Street towards the downs. It has not proved possible to identify any existing buildings, although many must remain. Cherhill still has many thatched cottages, but no remaining group like the one in the bottom right-hand corner.

A Fine Old Shakespearean House
With Oak Beams.
Throughout. Cherhill (5)

THIS FINE TIMBER-FRAMED HOUSE is now known as Deep Thatch. Its original name was Caswell's House and it is believed to have been built by a man named Caswell about 1770. Although known for many years as the Shakespearean House, as shown on the postcard, if the 1770 date is correct the house was built almost 200 years after Shakespeare's time. Built originally as a small farmhouse, it became two cottages and has now reverted to a single home.

THIS BUILDING, at the point where the A4 starts its climb onto the downs, was originally The Bell Inn, which is known to have existed in 1750. It did an important trade in the days when the A4 was the Bath Road carrying a heavy coach traffic between London, Bath and Bristol. It ceased to be an inn about 1872 and became Bell Farmhouse, and is now a private residence. It has unfortunately suffered in recent years from unsympathetic rendering and refenestration.

AN EARLY TWENTIETH-CENTURY VIEW looking from Cherhill towards the White Horse and the monument. Such shocks of corn were a characteristic feature of the harvest scene in the days before combine harvesters. The plantation of beeches above the White Horse was in its prime at the time this photograph was taken. The trees are thought to have been planted about 200 years ago and in recent years have suffered from old age, and more particularly from the great storm of 25 January 1990 when many of them were blown down.

THE CHERHILL WHITE HORSE was constructed in 1780 by Dr Christopher Alsop of Calne. He is reputed to have directed the operation of setting out the horse by shouting through a megaphone from a great distance. That the horse looks correctly proportioned from below, although its height is disproportionate to its length when seen from above, supports this story. The horse requires cleaning and rechalking from time to time. In former years this was done by the lord of the manor, in recent years through the activity of the people of Cherhill and local groups. During the Second World War the horse was covered over to prevent it providing a landmark for raiding aircraft.

AN AERIAL VIEW taken in the 1930s of the White Horse, the monument and Oldbury Camp. Oldbury Camp or Castle is a fine example of an Iron Age fortification dating from some time during the 800 years before the Roman invasion. The natural defensive site of the hilltop is surrounded by massive earth fortifications enclosing a total area of 25 acres.

THE WHITE HORSE, CHERHILL, CALNE.   G.4868.

A FINAL VIEW OF THE WHITE HORSE AND THE MONUMENT, taken from a card posted in 1953. The monument stands in the south-west corner of Oldbury Castle. It was erected in 1845 to the design of Charles Barry by the 3rd Marquess of Lansdowne in memory of his ancestor Sir William Petty who founded the family's fortunes. Oddly, there is no inscription on the monument to record the reason for its erection, which has led to erroneous speculation over the years. It stood on what was once the edge of Bowood land in that direction, but the site was no doubt chosen because of its prominence, as it is visible for thirty miles in some directions. The monument was recently acquired by The National Trust, which has undertaken its restoration, the work being half completed as this note is written.

THE VILLAGE BAKERY at Yatesbury owned by Mr Caswell, about 1936. It was just north of The Limers. All that remains today is the central building, now a private house. It is no longer thatched and has a modern extension to the left. Bourton Barn at the right has been replaced by a modern house.

THE BEECH AVENUE at Yatesbury, lining the road from the main road into the village, was a popular subject for photography, as in this Edwardian example.

A CARD OF YATESBURY posted in 1920 but almost certainly one of a pre-First World War series. The buildings at the centre were the bakery, illustrated on the previous page. The post office, run by Mr Abel and Mrs S.A. Shergold, was in the nearer cottages which have since been replaced.

A SLIGHTLY LATER VIEW OF THE AVENUE, taken nearer the church. A pony and trap are approaching and there is what may be a motor vehicle going away beyond it. It was posted on 11 October 1917. The cottages on the right are Vulpit Cottages near the church, which now look very different with a tiled roof and other alterations.

YATESBURY SHIRE STALLIONS-1936.

THE YATESBURY SHIRE STALLIONS in 1936. The stud was run on Nolands Farm and belonged to Cumbers of Theale, Berkshire. The photograph no doubt shows the whole strength of the stud and it may have been at or after its peak, as mechanization was making inroads into farming by the late 1930s.

A CLOSE-UP OF A GROUP OF STALLIONS held by two grooms. The stallions were taken in strings down to Calne railway station from where they were taken all over the West Country to serve mares on their farms, thereby maintaining the working horse population.

A CLOSE-UP of one of the magnificent Yatesbury shire stallions.

MR SAMUEL DOBLE on his hunter outside Nolands Farmhouse, Yatesbury. Sam's father moved from Somerset and farmed Nolands with his two sons. Sam served with horses during the First World War and later farmed at Cowage Farm, Hilmarton. He was a keen huntsman. The house no longer looks quite the same from this view because part of the rear wing has been demolished, so that only the front gable rather than a double gable can be seen.

AS WELL AS SHOWING A PICTURESQUE CORNER OF OLD CALSTONE, this is an interesting picture of a long lost local industry. The horse pulled the roller visible in the picture in a circle to crush the chalk stone stacked on the left into a powder from which whiting was made. Blocks of whiting were used, for example, to mark white lines on stone steps for smartness and safety. The premises were at the far end of the village and have now completely disappeared. The track on the left leads down to the waterworks.

Calstone (5)

ANOTHER PRE-FIRST WORLD WAR VIEW of a very rustic looking pair of cottages at Calstone. They were in the fields to the west of the church and all trace of them has now disappeared.

A CALSTONE SCHOOL GROUP about which the only information available is that it was taken before the 1920s. The large number of children in what is now a lightly-populated rural area is remarkable.

EQUALLY, THIS VIEW OF THE CALSTONE BAND in the 1920s indicates the number of men who may have been involved in agriculture in a small village at that time. Back row, left to right: C.W. Robbins, Leslie Dew, Arthur Barnett, E. Davis, -?-, Goodship(?), -?-. Front row: -?-, Fred Nichols (bandmaster), H. Goodship, -?-, Hubert Dew, Ted Dew.

THE FINE SILVER FLAGON of 1602 belonging to Heddington parish church, which sadly had to be sold to pay for renewal of the roof in the 1970s.

DESCRIBED ON THE CARD AS LOWER FARM, HEDDINGTON, this is now known as Home Farm. The card was posted on 11 May 1909 from Harry Pocock to a Mr Willis of Bulkington, near Devizes, saying 'We are expecting you tomorrow 1 o'clock', more evidence of reliance on the post in those days.

SECTION SIX

West and North of Calne: Sandy Lane to Bradenstoke

A CHARMING STUDY of Sandy Lane seen from the garden of The George Inn, probably in the 1940s, with Ann and Brian Vines, children of Percy (see page 132), in the foreground.

AN EDWARDIAN VIEW of Sandy Lane showing the track leading into Bowood Estate. The photographer has posed a postman on a three-wheeled velocipede to add interest. The card was posted on 24 August 1906.

A CARD IN THE SAME SERIES as the last showing a general view down the road at Sandy Lane looking towards Devizes. The cottage featured on the previous page is on the left.

ANOTHER VIEW OF ABOUT THE SAME PERIOD, this one on the opposite side of Bowood Park, showing the entrance gates at Derry Hill. A donkey cart stands outside the Reading Room and there is a horse and trap in the yard on the left.

Bowood House, Calne

THIS POSTCARD OF BOWOOD, posted in 1909, shows at right the Big House of the 1750s and '60s which was demolished in 1955 when it became uneconomic to maintain.

Bowood House (5) and Terraces.

Bowood, the seat of the Right Honourable the Marquess of Lansdowne, dates from the 13th century. It was partially rebuilt and added to by the famous architects, John and James Adam in 1754, the most distinctive portion of the house being, in part at least, a reproduction of a palace or villa in Dalmatia, used by the Roman Emperor Diocletian.

THIS CLOSER VIEW OF BOWOOD, perhaps taken a little later, shows from centre to left the Orangery designed in 1768 by Robert Adam and the older buildings behind it which form the present house. The terraces were laid out during the first half of the nineteenth century. The Orangery now contains a picture gallery and it and the terraces form the centre piece of Bowood Park which, with its grounds, adventure playground and other facilities, has in recent years become a very popular attraction, as well as remaining the home of the Earl and Countess of Shelburne.

A PRE-FIRST WORLD WAR VIEW of Bowood Park showing a herd of deer, which no longer exists, although there are a number of wild deer in the area.

A WINTRY VIEW OF BOWOOD LAKE. The Park, including the lake, was laid out for the first Marquess of Lansdowne by 'Capability' Brown in the 1760s.

NOTHING CAN BE ADDED to the written caption: 'Derry Hill Football Club: 1921–22'.

DERRY HILL POST OFFICE AND GARAGE in the 1920s. Mr Cyril H. Thomas ran both businesses at the time, and he went on to build up substantial garage and motor coach businesses in Chippenham and Calne.

HAZELAND FARM in the valley between Studley and Bremhill. The card was produced for advertising by R. Wood & Son, saying 'We are now booking turkeys for Christmas at 5/6 per pound dressed weight, at 5/- per pound clean plucked weight. Our turkeys are grass reared for top quality and flavour'. The card probably dates from the 1960s.

EXCAVATION OF THE FOUNDATIONS OF STANLEY ABBEY in the early years of the century. The abbey was founded for thirteen monks of the Cistercian order by Queen Matilda in 1151 at Lockswell, but moved down to the valley at Stanley three years later. It was destroyed on the dissolution of the monasteries in the sixteenth century and hardly a trace now remains.

THE RURAL PEACE of Ratford Hill in the early years of the century.

A PHOTOGRAPH OF ABOUT THE SAME PERIOD taken at the bottom of the hill, the carthorse being held by Frank Ponting (1884–1975).

THE DUMB POST INN at Bremhill has not changed greatly over the years, but this leafy view was probably taken forty or more years ago.

THIS EARLY POSTCARD of Bremhill Church was posted on 12 August 1904 in Chippenham bearing the message 'Dear sister, I am sending you the view of the dear old Church'. It was sent to Mrs Slade, Redfield, Bristol. Like most parish churches, Bremhill dates from many periods but includes much Early English work of about 1200 while the tower is probably fourteenth century.

A GROUP OF CHILDREN dressed in white, perhaps for a May Day celebration, by the entrance pillars to the vicarage at Bremhill. Undated, perhaps 1920s.

BREMHILL VICARAGE.

THE FORMER BREMHILL VICARAGE. This was an old house much altered by that eccentric Victorian, the Revd William Bowles, who was rector of Bremhill 1805–1844. He altered the façade to its present appearance and filled the garden with grottos, obelisks and the like, most of which have since disappeared.

The School and Cross (1) Bremhill.

THE SCHOOL AND CROSS outside the churchyard at Bremhill. The school is nineteenth-century and the cross is no doubt medieval. The stone steps are very heavily worn and the modern top cross shown in the picture has since disappeared.

NOTHING IS RECORDED of this group taken outside the school at Bremhill, apparently in the inter-war years. Readers may like to study the picture and try to decide what the children had been performing. The goose may indicate a connection with Mother Goose.

THE MAUD HEATH MONUMENT seen from the road at Wick Hill, Bremhill. Maud Heath died in 1474 leaving her estate in trust for the construction and maintenance of a footpath or 'causey' from Wick Hill to Chippenham. It has been maintained to this day and includes a section of pathway raised on brick arches where flooding occurs regularly at the River Avon crossing. The monument was erected in 1838 at the joint expense of the Trustees, Lord Lansdowne and the Reverend Bowles. The latter wrote the inscription: 'Thou, who do'st pause on this aerial height / Where MAUD HEATH'S Pathway winds in shade or light / Christian Way-farer, in a world of strife / Be still – and ponder on the path of life'. Pevsner commented, 'The quality of the poetry matches that of the statue'. The statue lost her head in the storm of 25 January 1990 but the Trustees replaced it in June 1990.

THE VIEW DOWN THE ROAD leading out of Bremhill to the east. The card was posted in September 1930.

AN EARLY TWENTIETH-CENTURY CARD of the school at Hilmarton with the village store on the right. Both buildings continue to perform the same function today. The school was built in 1851 at the expense of Thomas Poynder and was handed over to the County Council in 1914. All the buildings in the picture remain remarkably unchanged.

LOOKING SOUTH DOWN COMPTON ROAD at Hilmarton, probably in the 1920s. The buildings remain substantially unchanged, although one or two modern houses have been inserted. The cottages nearest the camera are dated 1832, the houses each side of the house with projecting porch are dated 1875 and of obvious Poynder Estate origin. The house with the porch is probably not as old as it looks, being rather Gothic Revival than medieval, and again is probably of Poynder Estate origin.

THE INTERIOR OF THE HILMARTON PARISH CHURCH OF ST LAURENCE. The nave is largely twelfth century, the Perpendicular-style screen of the fifteenth century and the chancel mainly Victorian.

Post Office, Hilmarton.

HILMARTON POST OFFICE early in the twentieth century. The house is dated 1876 and is of typical Poynder Estate style for its period.

A PRE-FIRST WORLD WAR photograph recorded as 'Lyneham people at Calne station'. The photographer has carefully obliterated the word 'Gentlemen' on the sign above the group.

A PICTURE OF LYNEHAM from the early years of the century, which modern readers will have difficulty in recognizing. It is in fact the main road looking towards Chippenham. The cottage in the distance is now fronted by a garage premises. The house on the right remains much as shown but the thatched cottages on the left have been altered almost out of recognition by modernization and re-roofing.

BRADENSTOKE VILLAGE, almost certainly taken between the wars. The Jolly Trooper on the right remains as shown. The cottage in the centre has been demolished and the inn's garden occupies its site. The cottages on the left have had their thatch replaced by a tiled roof.

A SOMEWHAT LATER VIEW, probably early post-war period, a little further down the street at Bradenstoke, again looking north. The houses shown remain, although considerably altered. In the distance is the building of mixed architectural styles called 'The Old Manor'. Next to it, the fine old jettied building remains, much of its timber frame now exposed and the far end in urgent need of attention. The pair of cottages nearest the camera on the left has been converted into one house, although the little porch seems to have been salvaged and moved to the new central door.

AN EARLY VIEW OF THE PRIORY FARMYARD at Bradenstoke. The building on the left with its Gothic windows may be the priory's tithe barn. On the right is a grain store built on staddle stones to keep out vermin. As to the fate of the barn, see the next page. No trace of the buildings in the picture can now be seen.

BRADENSTOKE WAS AN AUGUSTINIAN PRIORY founded in 1142. It was dissolved by Henry VIII in 1539 and by the twentieth century only the range of buildings on the west side of the cloister survived. They contained the guest house and the Prior's lodging; the western elevation is shown above.

THE EASTERN ELEVATION of the same building, the side on which the cloister once stood. The remains of the priory and the tithe barn were purchased in the 1930s by William Randolph Hearst and taken to St Donat's Castle in South Wales where he intended to re-erect them, but never did.

SECTION SEVEN

Matters Military

DURING THE FIRST WORLD WAR an aerodrome was established at Yatesbury. It is thought that this accident was caused by high winds. The planes may be Bristol BE 2e type of 1916.

A TROOP OF CAVALRY dismounted on The Strand, probably about the time of the First World War.

CAVALRYMAN GEORGE BUTCHER of the Blues and Royals. He was wounded at Passchendaele in 1917, when his horse was shot from under him, and is shown here convalescing at Bowood, where there was a war hospital, mounted on the Duke of Beaufort's horse.

THE CALNE VOLUNTEERS at camp, about 1897. Standing, first from the left, Cale Salde; fourth from the left, R.S. Heath, printer of Calne. Front row: second from the right, Steve Rumsey; standing, third from the right, Bert Buckeridge, who emigrated to California in 1900.

THIS CARD WAS POSTED in the reign of Edward VII but unfortunately the year is not clear. It was taken by Hunt of Calne and shows a cavalry camp, probably on the downs above Calne. The message says 'This was took at water last night, do you remember me and novelty'. Presumably Novelty was the writer's horse. Mr Hunt must have worked quickly to enable the sender to post the card the day after it was taken.

THE CALNE COMPANY OF HOME GUARD on the rifle range by the golf course below Morgan's Hill. On the extreme right is Mick Cook of the White Hart, Company Commander. Next to him Chris (?) Balch, Northern Platoon Commander. Extreme left is Cecil G. Higgins, Centre Platoon Commander. The rifle range is visible in the right background. The mobile kitchen bears the inscription 'Presented by The Canadian Red Cross Society to the Wiltshire Battalion Home Guard'.

B COMPANY, 1st Wilts. Home Guards outside the Woodlands at Calne.

THE FIRST WORLD WAR CAMP at Yatesbury. The inscription identifies the hospital of Number One Camp which is the building on the right, as evidenced by the lorry with red cross markings outside it. The officers' quarters are in the background and beyond them the clump of trees on Cherhill Down.

AN INTERIOR VIEW of one of the huts forming the First World War camp, this being the hut of 28 Squadron in Number One Camp, Yatesbury.

A GENERAL VIEW of the Royal Flying Corps Camp at Yatesbury. Biplanes parked on the grass can be dimly made out. Although Yatesbury hosted large camps in both world wars, all the buildings have been swept away and the land returned to agriculture, apart from two hangars and a few more permanent buildings such as the officers' mess.

A MONOPLANE in front of the hangars at Yatesbury. Believed to be a Morane Sulnier 'Parasol' LA type of 1916, 1 or 3 Squadron RFC.

A CLOSE-UP VIEW OF A BIPLANE at Yatesbury during the First World War. The photograph was sent with compliments from Second Lieutenant J.W. Shaw, 37 TDS. The plane is a Bristol F2B fighter with a Sunbeam Arab engine (about 1918).

ANOTHER UPENDED BIPLANE at Yatesbury during the First World War, again perhaps the result of high winds. This is probably an SE5 or SE5a of about 1917.

A SECOND WORLD WAR LIGHT TANK passes the bakery at Bremhill.

A RARE PHOTOGRAPH of the crew of an Eleventh Honourable Artillery Company tank during the desert campaign in North Africa during the Second World War. At the back is Ronald Ivor Butcher of Calne. The others came from all over the country. Left to right: Bombadier McVey, R.I.B., Gunner Gregson, Signaller Watson, Driver/mechanic Stephenson. The willow sticks strapped to the tank were cut from a sweet water canal and provided a framework for shade. The photograph was taken on 22 October 1942, the day before Alamein began.

Transport

CALNE SCOUTS of the 1950s with their trek cart. Brian Vines is nearest the camera.

BERT GOODENOUGH'S DONKEY GIG in his orchard at Compton Bassett with Lower End farmyard beyond. Frank Woodman is holding the donkey and the Goodenough children are sitting in the gig.

A FOUR-WHEELED DONKEY CARRIAGE outside Patford House in Patford Street at a time when it was still a private residence. It later became the offices of the Calne Borough Council and the Calne Town Council. The Town Council has quite recently moved into the Town Hall annexe but the North Wiltshire District Council still use part of the building as a local office.

A MILK CART IN SILVER STREET, Calne in 1914. It is driven by Ernest Rumming who used to drive in with milk from the Heanage Estate at Compton Bassett to deliver to the dairy which once existed behind 10 The Green.

ANOTHER OF THE REVEREND WHEELER'S PHOTOGRAPHS shows a loaded cart near the top of Ratford Hill going towards Bremhill. The cottage facing the camera still exists but the wing running parallel to the road has been demolished.

MR FRED FRY, baker of Bremhill, in his delivery cart. Note the light construction compared to the haulage carts on the previous page.

THE BOWOOD CARRIAGE standing outside Harper's in Wood Street, Calne, after being overhauled for the royal visit of 1907. Taylors' motor cycle premises now occupies the site. The picture was posted on 12 July 1907, two days after the royal visit, to Miss Lucy Chivers in Camborne, Cornwall 'with love from Fred'. It said nothing about the carriage or the royal visit but ended 'I have a good joke to tell you when I have time'.

CALNE RAILWAY COMPANY.

NOTICE.

CALNE AMATEUR DRAMATIC SOCIETY.

A

SPECIAL TRAIN

WILL LEAVE

CHIPPENHAM

For CALNE, at 11.30. p.m., on February 22nd, 1881, for the
convenience of Persons attending the

ENTERTAINMENT,

To be given the same Evening, by the above Society, at the

Town Hall, Chippenham.

Fares at the usual prices.

EDWARD R. HENLY,
Secretary.

17th February, 1881.

A. HEATH AND SON, PRINTERS, CALNE.

THIS POSTER IS A STRIKING TESTIMONY to the strength of local enterprise in the nineteenth century. Here we have the Calne Railway Company running a special train from Chippenham to Calne at 11.30 p.m. for people who had been attending the Calne Amateur Dramatic Society performance in Chippenham. The poster was printed by Heath in Calne. The Calne Railway Company was absorbed by the Great Western Railway Company in 1892.

THIS CARD was inscribed simply. 'To Ethel from Percy Christmas 1920'. Local enquiry revealed that the smart young GWR porter was Percy Vines, then aged seventeen. He worked on the railway for nearly fifty years and still lives in Calne. Ethel, now aged ninety-three, was his cousin.

STANLEY BRIDGE HALT on the Chippenham to Calne Branch. The halt (then spelt halte) was opened about two miles from Chippenham on 3 April 1905 when the Great Western Railway introduced steam railcars on the branch. The photograph is taken looking towards Chippenham and the bridge in the background carries the Pewsham to Bremhill Road.

CALNE STATION STAFF of the 1920s, taken at the top of Station Road just outside the station.

A GATHERING OF THE STAFF at Calne Station with a presentation being made in the 1950s, by station master Percy Gleed to retiring foreman Horace Poole. Left to right: G. Tanner, C. Skull, J. Whiles, E. Ponting, T. Moore, -?-, K. Kitt, B. Sage, J. Kington, R. Howell, Ann Vines (see page 101), Frank Brittain, P. Harris. Behind are signalman A. Iles with dog and permanent way staff.

The G.W.R. Station, Calne.

AN EDWARDIAN VIEW of Calne Station. Tall milk churns which once provided a great deal of traffic are much in evidence.

CALNE STATION in the last days of the passenger service with the diesel multiple unit train standing at the platform. The canopy has been extended right up to the end of the platform since the photograph at top was taken. Entrance to the goods yard is on the left with a corner of the by then disused goods shed showing. All sidings had been removed and the signal box in the background was out of use. The Calne Railway Company opened the line in 1863. Under the Beeching closures, freight services were withdrawn in October 1964 and the passenger service on 18 September 1965. The station site has been obliterated by a small industrial estate.

THIS IS SAID TO BE THE FIRST MOTOR MOWER USED IN CALNE, at the home of Mrs Harris, The Grange, Curzon Street (now Springfield School). The photograph is recorded as having been taken in 1920.

A YOUNG MEMBER OF THE BLACKFORD FAMILY showing off an early motor cycle on the hill in Brewers Lane between Anchor Road and Shelburne Road. In the background can be seen the river Marden impounded to drive Swaddon's Mill in Horsebrook. The initials B & S on the tank are believed to stand for Barr & Stroud, a very small, obscure producer, and the date is about 1912.

A 1920S PICTURE OF TWO STEAM LORRIES standing in Wessington Avenue. The second has a name on the top board which may be Reeve and it certainly ends with Calne. Such steam lorries were much used locally before the general introduction of motor lorries.

A GROUP OF WORKERS from the Co-operative Wholesale Society's estate at Compton Bassett photographed on an outing by lorry in 1925. The Roe Buck Inn may be in Salisbury. The driver is Harry Evans. The lorry is probably an Albion of the 1915–20 period.

OUTSIDE THE STABLE BLOCK OF COMPTON HOUSE in 1925 is the lorry used by the CWS for milk deliveries, with driver Jim Rumming. The truck is a Ford, again of the 1915–20 period.

BY WAY OF CONTRAST, this splendid vehicle was photographed outside the front of Compton House in 1913. Colonel Drake was tenant of the house at the time. It is difficult to be specific as to the make of the motor because coach builders of the time built onto different manufacturer's chassis. It may be a Mercedes.

THE ONLY CERTAIN CALNE CONNECTION of this photograph is that it was taken by Messrs Bolt and Pike of Calne. It was taken at the top of Bowden Hill above Lacock, as is proved by the small lock-up or blind house in the background. The author's attention has been drawn to the book *Lacock – Recollections of life in the Wiltshire Village*, edited by Peter Murray, which reproduces this picture with the comment 'One of the first cars in the area owned by Sir John Gladstone from Bowden Park. The first to come through the village, according to Edward Brinkworth, was one owned by Mr H. Harris, son of Thomas Harris of Harris's Bacon Factory at Calne'. Perhaps Sir John Gladstone and Mr Harris united for this photograph of early motoring. The cars are of the period 1908–10 and are probably an Austin and a Ford.

A PLEASANT IMPRESSION OF MOTORING in the 1920s is given by this photograph of Mr Raymond Angell of Back Road, Calne and his family at Derry Hill. The car is a Morris Cowley of about 1920.

MR AND MRS BERTRAM SPACKMAN display their decorated car in 1926. In view of the imperial theme it was probably decorated for an Empire Day Procession. Mr Spackman was a solicitor practising in the town and Mrs Edith Mary Spackman was briefly Calne's first lady mayor in 1937. The decoration makes identification of the car difficult but it is probably an A.C. or bullnose Morris.

CALNE CARNIVAL, 1926. Mock bride and groom represented by Gwendoline Ponting of Bremhill, who later went to live in Florida, and Mr Leslie Fry of Bremhill, well known for his glass engravings, then aged nine. The chauffeur was Tom Pickett of Oxford Road who had a taxi business at the time. His wife was headmistress of Bremhill School for many years. The car is a Ford.

THE DAUGHTER OF MR HEWLETT of Home Farm (page 72) married the head gardener at Highclere House, Berkshire, which was owned by Lord Carnarvon, best known as the discoverer of Tutankhamun. The connection resulted in this trip of Compton Bassett people in a charabanc hired from Haddrell's of Calne, photographed somewhere *en route* for Highclere, perhaps at Newbury.

CLEARING SNOW from the road over the downs from Calne to Devizes in the early post-war period, probably in the great freeze of 1947.

Commerce and Industry

MR ALBERT ('BERT') GOODENOUGH in his yard at Compton Bassett about 1930. It is interesting to see that the donkey cart was still in use at such a late date. See his bill heading on page 84.

THIS OLD PHOTOGRAPH seemed to show a group of butchers at the Harris factory but there was no information at all with it. It was published in the *Wiltshire Gazette & Herald*, and as a result the author heard from Mrs Daphne Hardwick who identified her great uncle George Summers, second right in the front row. He was chief butcher at Harris's at about the time of the photograph, earning 18s. a week, and his gang would slaughter 400 pigs before breakfast. He died about 1960 in his eighties, which would place the photograph in the early 1900s. Mr Summers was born at Freeth Farm, Compton Bassett and later became a farmer and potato merchant at Lickhill, Calne.

CALNE SHOPPING WEEK EXHIBITION in the Town Hall, 1926. The blackboard on the left at the back bears the chalk message 'Sent specially from London'.

WHITE HART HOTEL, CALNE, Family and Commercial.

AN ADVERTISEMENT for the White Hart Hotel on the junction of London Road and The Green, from a pre-First World War town guide.

THIS LITTLE SHOP at Lower Quemerford was demolished to provide the entrance to the Wessington Park housing development in the 1960s.

AT ONE TIME there was another Buckeridge shop in Calne, the jewellers which still exists in High Street, owned by Walter Buckeridge in the early years of the century until he emigrated to Perth, Western Australia in 1911. The photograph shows the gas lamps erected to illuminate the window display from the outside, a popular arrangement at the time.

A LATER PHOTOGRAPH of the same shop when it had passed into the ownership of Bridges.

Calne Co-operative Society, Ltd.

(Registered under the "Industrial & Provident Societies' Act, 1893.")

Grocers, Bakers, Confectioners,
Provision Merchants, &c.

Registered Office and Stores :—

THE SQUARE, CALNE.

Dividend paid on all purchases in addition to five per cent Interest on Share Capital invested in the Society.

Profits divided half-yearly

⁎⁎⁎ Visitors to the Town and Neighbourhood, and especially intending residents, always welcomed.

ANOTHER PAGE from the pre-First World War guide, showing the Co-op in The Square at Calne. The buildings shown were unfortunately demolished in the 1930s to make way for the unattractive white-faced building which still stands on the site, although no longer owned by the Calne Co-operative Society (see *Greetings from Calne* : 77 and 78).

DIXONS' WINDOW DISPLAY in their shop in Church Street, Calne for Shopping Week 1926. A fascinating selection of contemporary ladies' wear.

FREDERICK C. HUNT'S FOOTWEAR SHOP. No detail is provided with the photograph but it is almost certainly contemporary with the one above and shows Mr Hunt's display for Shopping Week 1926.

THIS PHOTOGRAPH FROM THE INTER-WAR YEARS shows a young lady bedecked with Harris advertising, with a strong patriotic appeal. She was probably dressed for a carnival procession.

THESE LITTLE STICKERS can still occasionally be found on old items of furniture. The prices are astonishing in comparison to what one has to pay in an antique shop for such comparatively ordinary items of domestic furniture today. The table is priced from 10s. (50p), the armchair from 7s. 3d. (36p) and the plain chair from 2s. 10d. (14p).

EDWARD W. MAUNDRELL,

❖ ENGINEER, ❖

CALNE, WILTSHIRE, ENGLAND.

Improved Gas Pig-Singeing Apparatus.

This Apparatus consists of a semi-cylindrical shield or chamber, embracing the body of the Pig; it is furnished on the inside with a number of gas jets, and also with air tubes to propel the gas against the animal. The Apparatus is suspended by a chain passing over pulleys and balanced by a weight, enabling the Assistant to raise or depress it with ease.

The advantages over the use of Straw are very many.

There is no smell or smoke.

The flame can be so managed as to apply it to any part instantly, and can be put out in a moment.

There are no blacks left, as with straw.

There is a great saving of time.

There is no risk of Fire or explosion.

The cost, compared with Straw, is not one-eighth the amount.

Price of Singer only	...	...	...	...	£10 0 0
Singer, with hand-power Fan, Hose pipes for air and gas, &c., fixed complete		...	...	...	£20 0 0

EDWARD W. MAUNDRELL took over the Horsebrook premises as his foundry in 1885 after running an iron works for five years in what became the Primitive Methodist chapel in London Road.

ANOTHER MAUNDRELL'S PRODUCT for the bacon industry, a lard press. The *Pictorial Record* of October 1898 recorded 'As a general engineer Mr Maundrell can turn out anything, from a steam engine to a pig trough; but it is as a designer and manufacturer of agricultural machinery, bacon-curing appliances and lard-rendering plant that he is best known'.

CALNE MUNICIPAL ELECTION.

To the Burgesses of the Borough of Calne.

Ladies and Gentlemen,

I have been nominated as a Candidate for the Municipal Election which has been done without my consent and against my wish; being from home on Wednesday last I was unable to state my objections and get my name withdrawn.

My reason for not seeking re-election is because I have found it very difficult to spare the time which I consider is necessary to properly carry out the duties of a Councillor, and, should I be elected, I feel I should be keeping another out who would be better fitted for the seat than myself.

Therefore I have no alternative but to ask the Electors to leave my name out and to make their selection from the other candidates.

Apologising for thus troubling you,

I am, Ladies and Gentlemen,

Your obedient Servant,

EDWARD W. MAUNDRELL.

Printed and Published by R. S. Heath, Strand, Calne, Wilts.

A RATHER AMUSING HANDBILL in which Mr Maundrell withdrew his nomination as candidate for the Borough Council. The author has a copy of another handbill, dated 1896, in which Mr Maundrell thanked the electors for his election to the Council, so it is likely that his withdrawal notice dates from about 1900. He must have been a busy man. His foundry employed more than thirty people and he was honorary captain of the Calne Fire Brigade.

☞ 1886 ☜

Illustrated ✠ Price ✠ List

OF

"PARAGON" SPRING CHEESE PRESSES,

CENTRAL-AXLE BACK-ACTION HAYMAKERS,

AND OTHER MACHINERY,

MANUFACTURED BY

MAUNDRELL & WOODWARD,

ENGINEERS, IRON FOUNDERS, MILLWRIGHTS, &c.,

THE FOUNDRY,

CALNE, WILTSHIRE, ENGLAND.

Sold by

MAUNDRELL'S 1886 LEAFLET, illustrating a hay turner or 'tedder'.

SECTION TEN

Agriculture

BUILDING A RICK AT ABBEY FARM, Stanley about 1920 when everything was done by horse and muscle. The elevator was probably made by Maundrell and it is powered by the windlass in the left foreground, worked by the horse in traces on the left with a little girl sitting on it. No doubt she was put there for the photograph. The horse was probably left to work of its own accord.

OXEN WERE USED ON FARMS IN THE AREA until the beginning of this century, when this team was photographed in the Cherhill or Calstone area by the Revd Wheeler.

THREE HORSES IN LINE pulling a plough at Compton Bassett, with ploughman Jim Rumming assisted by ploughboy Frank Woodman.

ANOTHER PHOTOGRAPH AT CUMBER'S STUD at Yatesbury, with a groom running up a great shire stallion, the feathers on his fetlocks flying.

RURAL CALNE OF THE EARLIER YEARS OF THE CENTURY. A horse-drawn hayrake in the northern part of the town, probably in the area of Penn Hill Drive with Penn Hill in the background.

ANOTHER VIEW OF THE WHITE HORSE at Cherhill looking across a field with shocks of corn, and in the foreground a typical horse-drawn Wiltshire wagon used for carrying the corn, its riggers fitted to increase the straw-carrying capacity.

A CLASSIC SCENE OF STEAM THRASHING on Whitley Farm, Calne, with Edward Maundrell's tackle, the traction engine supplied by a horse-drawn water cart. The farm belonged to Mr Charles Henry Freeth Vines and he and his wife and daughter Diana are in the photograph. The *Pictorial Record* already mentioned commented 'Mr Maundrell hires out reaping-and-binding machines, mowing machines and thrashing tackle on a very extensive scale, and has a great array of this class of appliances'. Traction engines were to be seen working thrashing machines until after the Second World War but tractors replaced them before thrashing machines in turn were largely replaced by combine harvesters.

ANOTHER PHOTOGRAPH OF WHITLEY FARM with Mr Vines and his wife Florence Ruth ploughing by tractor. The tractor is a 1917 24 hp 'Overtime' from Waterloo Boy, USA. They were imported to help overcome the labour shortage during the First World War and were among the earliest tractors used in this country. After their retirement, Mr and Mrs Vines lived for many years at Adam House, The Green, Calne.

ANOTHER EXAMPLE of an agricultural vehicle manufactured by Edward Maundrell, this being a liquid manure tank transporter for horse haulage.

HAYMAKING IN 1919 with a Maundrell elevator at the top of Compton Hill. Part of the Co-operative Wholesale Society's workforce. They are, left to right: Bill Rumming, Jack Rumming, Jack Fell, Jim Rumming, Frank Matthews and John Butler.

MORE RURAL CALNE, this time showing Mr Burchell with his sons shooting in a potato field at Lickhill Gardens about 1920. The North End – Braemor Road housing estates now occupy this area.

PEA PICKING AT SANDS FARM, Calne in the mid-1920s, when it was farmed by Mr R. Kenneth Henly, father of Henly Brothers who still farm it. Left to right, Mrs 'Fan' Fisher, Alma Rumming, Mrs Taylor and Jack Rumming.

A SUPERB STUDY OF STEAM THRASHING on Manor Farm, Calstone. The farm then as now was farmed by the Maundrell family, at that time by Joseph Hill Maundrell, standing centre in front of the driving belt. He was killed by lightning at Calstone on 5 May 1926, aged fifty-six. The picture is full of wonderful detail and repays study. Note, for example, from the left, the wooden wheelbarrow and wooden farm cart with heavy horse to carry the grain in sacks behind it to the barn. The carter and others in the picture have their trouser legs rigged to keep out rats. Behind the thrashing machine is an elevator, no doubt by Maundrell, feeding to the top of a very large rick. Bags of grain are hanging on the front of the machine. The

machine sifted the grain into different grades, hence the multiplicity of sacks. The pitchers are near the bottom of the rick behind the engine but there seem to be more untouched ricks, thatched with straw, awaiting attention behind the thrashing machine. The steam engine was portable, i.e. not self-propelled like a traction engine but having to be hauled. The horse shafts for hauling it are lying on the ground in the foreground. Brown & May of Devizes built machines of this sort and the cylinder detail looks like theirs. On the right is a wooden bowser to feed the engine with water, with a trough between it and the engine, from which the engine drew its supply.

ACKNOWLEDGEMENTS

I have been able to write this book only because of the great deal of help I have received from other people. My thanks go to everyone who has provided photographs, and information about them. If I have omitted the name of anyone to whom I am indebted I ask them to accept my apologies and I also accept responsibility for any mistakes which have crept in. Pencilled notes on the backs of photographs do not always provide reliable information.

I owe a particular debt for the provision of photographs and information to Mr Graham Tanner, local correspondent of the *Wiltshire Gazette & Herald*, who has published many fascinating photographs of old Calne in his column over the years. I am also especially grateful to Mr John Buckeridge, who has assembled a wonderful collection of Calne memorabilia from which have come some of the best old photographs used in this book. I have mentioned in the Introduction the excellent exhibition of village records held at Compton Bassett and I would like to thank Mr Reg Rumming and Mr John Reis for helping me to obtain the copies required. I am also indebted to the Wiltshire Archaeological and Natural History Society and its librarian Mrs Pamela Colman for allowing me the use of a number of copyright pictures from its library at Devizes, the excellent photographs of Bradenstoke Priory being of particular interest.

Others to whom I give my thanks are in alphabetical order:

Mr G. Barber • the late Mr D.G. Blackford • Mr P.A. Brown (Town Clerk)
Mr Paul Buckeridge • Mr R.I. Butcher • Calne Antiques (Mr Malcolm Blackford)
Calne Town Council • Mrs Fenwick • Mrs S. Ferris • Mr L. Fry
Miss Joyce Green • Mr P.L. Gowar • Mrs D. Hardwick • Mr Richard Higgins
Mrs M. Hillier • Mr John Lambourne • Mr Michael Maundrell
Mr and Mrs W. Parry • Mr Ashley Ponting • Paul Ricketts • Mrs S.J. Sidelnik
Mr C.J. Thomas • Mr Percy Vines • Mr C. and Mrs K. Warner
The Misses M. and W. Wheeler • Mr and Mrs J. Whiles • Miss Patricia Wiltshire.

Books I have consulted include:

Calne in Camera, Calne Borough Council, 1974; *Calne in Pictures*, Calne Town Council, 1982; *Calne in Focus*, Calne Town Council, 1984; *Greetings from Calne*, Calne Town Council, 1988; *A History of the Borough and Town of Calne*, A.E.W. Marsh, published by Robert S. Heath in Calne, 1903; *The Manor and Village of Cherhill*, J.H. Blackford, 1941; *The Calne Branch*, Graham Tanner, Oxford Publishing Co., 1972; *The Wilts. & Berks. Canal*, L.J. Dalby, The Oakwood Press, 1986; *St Mary's School, Calne*, K. Stedmond, 1986; *White Horses and Other Hill Figures*, Maurice Marples, Alan Sutton, 1981; *Bowood Guide Book*; *The Buildings of England: Wiltshire*, Nikolaus Pevsner, Penguin Books, 1963; *Calne Town Guide*, Calne Town Council, British Publishing Co., 1989.

Finally, my thanks to those who have helped me in the production of the book, Mr Derek Parker for photographic work, my secretary Mrs Janet Bruce for typing and re-typing the manuscript, and my wife for her help and support throughout.